First Steps in
Vegetarian
Cooking

KATHY SILK

Illustrations by Melanie Andrews

Published by
The Vegetarian Society of the United Kingdom Ltd
Parkdale, Dunham Road, Altrincham
Cheshire WA14 4QG

© Copyright
The Vegetarian Society (UK) Ltd 1979

ISBN 0 900774 14 2

Printed by Joseph Ward & Co (Printers) Ltd
Wesley Place, Wellington Road, Dewsbury
West Yorkshire WF13 1HR

QUESTIONS YOU MIGHT WELL ASK!

WHY don't some folk eat meat, fish or fowl?

WHO are these people?

WHAT do they eat instead?

HOW should **I** go about it?

WHEN shall I try?

WHERE can I turn for help?

CONTENTS

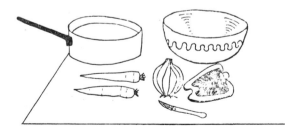

WELL, WHY DON'T SOME FOLK EAT MEAT, FISH OR FOWL?

There are many reasons—here are a few.

Many people find that eating dead flesh is repugnant to them.

Others query the morality of taking life for food. Some have only just discovered the horrors of factory-farming and want no further part of it.

Some have realised that, if they couldn't kill an animal or bird themselves for food, they shouldn't pay someone else to do the dirty work for them.

Still more feel that they only want to consume natural, wholesome, clean food to improve and maintain their personal health.

If you have not yet read *Food for a Future* by Jon Wynne-Tyson and *Animal Liberation* by Peter Singer, please do—soon! They are obtainable from The Vegetarian Society whose address is at the back of the book.

WHO ARE THESE PEOPLE? WHAT ARE THEY LIKE?

JUST LIKE YOU AND ME

They are thinking, caring people who want to help lessen the unnecessary cruelty and exploitation of animals . . . with the added bonus of improving their own health.

In the past Pythagoras, Socrates, Leonardo da Vinci, Milton, Voltaire, Shelley, Wordsworth, Isaac Pitman, Tolstoy, Mr & Mrs Bramwell Booth, Mahatma Gandhi, Bernard Shaw were advocates of vegetarianism.

Today we have Lord Brockway, Brigid Brophy, Sir Clifford Curzon, Lady Dowding, Beryl Grey, Arthur Latham MP, Malcolm Muggeridge, William Price MP, Richard Ryder, Sir Barnes Wallis, Bernard Weatherill MP.

WHAT DO THEY EAT INSTEAD?

All the delicious things that come from the earth: fruits, vegetables, pulses (beans, peas, lentils, chick peas etc.) nuts, seeds (sesame, sunflower, pumpkin), salads, whole grains (wholemeal bread, wholegrain brown rice, wholewheat spaghetti, macaroni etc).

Textured soya foods, cheese and other milk products, free range eggs and plantmilks are also used by some to add to the above range of foods.

Why eat these particular things?
Because we like good value for money.
Because we think it is pointless filling your stomach with 'empty calorie' food when you could be eating well and increasing your health, feeling and looking fitter.

HOW SHOULD I GO ABOUT IT?

Start by having a ϒ Day once a week.
ϒ for Vegetarian Day, that is!

Then go on to two ϒ Days a week a little later, increasing at your own rate.

Begin the day with a small glass ($\frac{1}{4}$ pint) of natural unsweetened orange, grapefruit or pineapple juice, *OR* eat a fresh orange or grapefruit.

Make a fruity muesli—there are many variations (see page 42).

Then have a slice of wholemeal bread or a roll, spread preferably with vegetable margarine, or with butter or peanut butter; add a thin spread of yeast extract (Barmene or Tastex) or marmalade (made with dark sugar); *OR* have either mushrooms, beans or tomatoes on wholemeal toast.

Lunch   —For packed lunch ideas for school, workplace or when travelling, picnics etc. see page 13.
    —For those at home see page 16.
Evening meal—For a variety of interesting recipes see page 24

WHEN SHALL I TRY?

Why not get ready today for your first Ƴ Day tomorrow?

What you need in your store cupboard to start with:
Breakfast: Either fresh, canned, bottled fruit juice or fruit.

A muesli base—i.e. a mixture of several cereals or just rolled oats, or a wholewheat product, such as Weetabix or Shredded Wheat.

Either a ½lb bag of mixed shelled nuts or 2 or 3 smaller bags of shelled nuts of the type you like.

1lb dark brown sugar—Barbados, Muscovado or real Demerara Sugar.

½lb dried untreated fruit—raisins, sultanas, dates etc.

Fresh fruit for slicing or grating into the muesli.

Milk, milk powder, dried or tinned liquid plantmilk.

Wheatgerm (Bemax, Froment etc.) if liked.

Natural bran (if required).

Wholemeal bread or rolls.

Vegetable margarine or butter.

Jar of Barmene, Tastex or Marmite yeast extract.

Real peanut butter (without preservatives) from a health food or wholefood store, where you can also obtain muesli base, nuts, dark sugar, granogen (soya milk powder), Plamil (liquid plantmilk), wheatgerm, bran etc.

Most of these items will last for many Ƴ Day breakfasts.

9

Lunch and Evening Meal

Choose ideas and recipes from each section, and check to see if you have the appropriate items in store. If not, list them after your breakfast ones, and head for the shops!

ϒ DAY GUIDELINES

When choosing food for yourself or your family, it's as well to bear the following in mind:

The more raw food you eat, the more vitamins, minerals, and roughage you will obtain for your better health; in other words, a large raw salad daily with a protein savoury is best for everyone.

When you cook vegetables, use only a little water, little or no salt, and short-cook them; or steam or bake them. You may be surprised at the good natural flavour that has previously been masked by salt and lost by over-cooking. Either drink the cooking liquid or keep covered in a refrigerator for up to 24 hours only and use in sauces, soups or casseroles. The minerals from the vegetables are in the water—don't waste them by throwing it away. Don't peel root vegetables—just scrub them well before cooking.

If you can grow some of your own vegetables, salads, fruit and herbs on natural composted soil, so much the better.

Use wholemeal bread and flour—it's tastier and more satisfying. If you have not already tried making your own bread, have a go using the recipe on page 47.

Wholegrain brown rice is tastier and more nutritious than white. Although there are mineral traces in all 'dark' sugars—but none at all in white—use very sparingly anyway.

If you have as great a variety as you can of these natural wholesome foods, as suggested in this book, obtaining the best quality you can afford, preparing the fresh ones just before use, short-cooking where required, and making your meals look attractive as well as taste delicious, you will benefit enormously from the change to ϒ Day eating.

We like to use 100% vegetable oil—corn oil, sunflower oil, sesame oil, olive oil, soya oil, etc. for cooking and making salad dressings.

We like to use 100% vegetable margarine or butter for spreading and some cooking. 100% vegetable white fats, such as Trex and Silver Standard Pura for cooking are now widely available. We do not use lard, suet, dripping or animal-based white cooking fats.

We like to use agar agar or carragheen moss (Gelozone) for making savoury or sweet jellies. Prepared fruit jellies, needing only fruit juice or water to be added, can be obtained at health food stores. We do not use gelatine or the usual jelly blocks, which are made from animal bones and hides.

We like to use free range eggs instead of battery farm eggs. These are not obtainable everywhere, and are usually more expensive, but you may find some by repeated requests and checking the actual source yourself. Some smallholdings often keep a few free range hens; it would be worth while trying to find one in your own locality.

We like to use vegetable stock cubes (concentrated flavour with minerals from vegetables) which can be bought at health food stores and some supermarkets; and don't use the so-called 'meaty' ones commonly available. Home-made stock is easily made by boiling well-washed outside leaves of cabbage etc for 30 minutes, straining and using the liquid for soups, casseroles and savoury sauces.

At the time of going to press the branded products referred to in this book were completely vegetarian in content. However, no guarantees can be given that they remain so and reference to the Shoppers' Guide section of the International Vegetarian Healthfood Handbook is advised.

11

METRIC CONVERSION

The weights and measures used in this book can be converted to grammes and litres on the following basis:

1oz	= 25-30 grammes
4oz	= 100-120 grammes
8oz ($\frac{1}{2}$lb)	= 225 grammes

$\frac{1}{2}$ pint	= 300 millilitres (ml) = just over $\frac{1}{4}$ litre
1 pint	= 600 ml = just over $\frac{1}{2}$ litre
$1\frac{3}{4}$ pints	= 1 litre

PACKED LUNCHES

for school, workplace, travelling or picnics

May I suggest that you pack a salad separately in a polybag or plastic box—with a mini-fork—as most salad items spoil very quickly between slices of bread.

Try scrubbed carrot sticks, crisp raw cauliflower florets, lettuce hearts, small firm tomatoes, spring onions, chunky sticks of green pepper, celery, endive or chicory, chunks of cucumber, radishes. By simply washing any of these items quickly in the morning and popping in the bag or box, instead of shredding or chopping them, you will be helping to preserve their vitamins.

Always prepare salad items just before you are going to eat or pack them. Don't leave any kind of green or root vegetables, for salad or cooking, soaking in water for long periods before use; you could be leaving vital elements behind in the water.

Make a wholemeal sandwich or roll to eat with your salad, filled with one of the many suggestions overleaf. They are easy to make, and all you need are a small bowl, a fork, spoon and small wire sieve.

To complete your meal, take a piece of fresh fruit—apple, pear, orange, etc—or one of the wrapped Fruit and Nut Bars (see page 15). These bars can be individually wrapped in clearfilm, and stored in a tin in a cool place for about two weeks.

HOME-MADE PASTES FOR SPREADING

Simply mash together your chosen ready grated or chopped ingredients, along with a little softened margarine or oil, until a fairly smooth paste is obtained; taste, adjust if necessary, cover with lid or clearfilm, and place in cold corner or refrigerator until required. Don't leave it there longer than 24 hours!

Most of these spreads can be made the evening before for morning-rush spreading!

A few spoonfuls of any kind of left-over beans with tomato pulp and herbs of choice.

Cream cheese, chopped chives and finely chopped raw mushrooms.

Finely-grated cheddar cheese with grated raw or cooked beetroot.

Peanut butter with either chopped celery or onion rings or fresh chopped herbs or mashed banana.

Cream cheese, chopped pineapple pieces with a little mint.

Finely-grated cheddar cheese, mashed dates and grated orange rind.

Finely-ground hazelnuts, tomato pulp, pinch of basil herb.

Slices of home-made nutroast (see page 24) with chutney.

Home-made lentil paste (see page 15) with chopped onion.

Tartex paste or Granose sandwich spread (from health food stores) with finely-ground nuts.

Lentil Paste

Put 4oz of washed and picked-over lentils into a pan with $\frac{1}{2}$ pint of water. Add a small peeled onion with a bayleaf pinned to it by two cloves (a studded onion), put on lid, bring to boil, turn down to simmer point for about 15-20 minutes when the water should have boiled away and the lentils be soft and fluffy. Remove onion (use for soup, without cloves), add an ounce of vegetable margarine, pinch of nutmeg, little salt, and 1 tablespoonful of finely-chopped parsley. Blend all together until smooth. Spoon into a basin, cool and cover before placing in the refrigerator. It will be quite firm by morning, and is also sliceable to go with salad for a quick lunch at home. A little curry powder or horse-radish powder, or a pinch of dried herbs, or chopped fresh herbs will add variety to this and other pastes.

A paste for spreading may also be made from split yellow peas, split green peas, whole green dried peas, chick peas, and any kind of bean, by soaking in cold water after washing well, for up to 12 hours prior to cooking. The cooking time varies from just over an hour for the split peas, to possibly two hours for chick peas, most kinds of bean and whole dried green peas. Black-eyed beans are one exception; they don't need soaking and are cooked in 30 to 40 minutes.

Fruit and Nut Bars

6oz finely-chopped dates
6oz finely-chopped dried apricots
2oz finely-ground cashews
2oz finely-ground hazels
Grated rind and juice of small orange

Method:
Blend all ingredients with a wooden spoon or fork, or put through a mincer. Flatten mixture into a tin, lined with rice paper, to $\frac{1}{2}$ inch thickness and press another sheet on top; leave to set. Cut into squares with a hot sharp knife.

15

Any dried fruit or nuts can be used for these delicious little bars—for example, prunes, raisins, currants, sultanas, dried apples, pears or bananas, almonds, walnuts. By coarse-grating some of the nuts you will make the bars more crunchy.

A mouli-mill, with a coarse and a fine drum made from stainless steel, is available in many shops; this is very useful indeed for grinding nuts, cheese, carrots, breadcrumbs and chocolate.

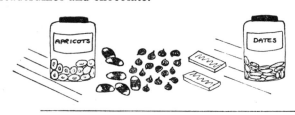

QUICK LUNCHES AT HOME

If you are lunching alone, try to have one of the following dishes or similar—don't go without or have an unbalanced meal just because it seems too much bother for one. Over a long period, this can play havoc with your health. These mini-meals are very easy to put together, and some are quite inexpensive.

Cheese and Brown Rice Savoury (for four)

4oz washed brown rice
1oz vegetable margarine
6oz grated cheddar cheese
2 tbsp finely-chopped parsley
$\frac{1}{4}$lb lightly-fried chopped mushrooms
Seasoning

Method:
Steam rice over boiling water until cooked. Place in basin with the margarine, cheese, parsley, fried mushrooms and seasoning. Stir well so that cheese binds everything together as it melts. Serve immediately with a fresh green salad. Can be chilled and then cut into squares.

Ratatouille (for four)

1 large aubergine
2 large peppers, green and red
2 large onions
5 large tomatoes, peeled
1lb marrow, courgettes or cucumber
1 clove garlic, peeled and crushed
6 tbsp corn oil
Salt, pepper and sugar
2 tbsp chopped parsley

Method:

Cube aubergine, sprinkle with salt, leave for 30 minutes, then squeeze out and discard the juice which may be bitter. Crush garlic, peel and slice onions, peppers, tomatoes and courgettes. Heat oil, add vegetables, stir carefully, put lid on pan and cook over very low heat for 30 minutes. Season and add a little sugar. Serve with parsley sprinkled over.

Makes a meal when served with wholemeal bread and cheese, and can be eaten either hot or cold.

Cheese and Apple Toast for One

Grate 2oz cheddar cheese and mix with a grated dessert apple. Toast a slice of wholemeal bread on one side only, spoon mixture on to the untoasted side and put under the grill until the cheese is melted. Arrange slices of raw tomato across the toast and surround with watercress.

Toasted wholemeal bread spread with a savoury bean or nut paste, topped with grilled mushrooms or tomatoes, or onion rings and a cress and cucumber salad is also quick to prepare.

OR Soya beans in tomato sauce, baked beans or curried baked beans on wholemeal toast and a green salad.

Welsh Rarebit Special

Stir a pinch of dry mustard powder into 2 tablespoonfuls of milk in a pan and add 2oz grated cheddar cheese; stir well over gentle heat until melted. Add a chopped tomato and chopped spring onion; spoon on to hot toast and surround with cress or lettuce.

Spaghetti Neapolitan

Boil 2oz wholewheat spaghetti in a little water with a teaspoon of vegetable oil and a pinch of salt. Meanwhile, fry a small chopped onion, add either two fresh tomatoes chopped or a small tin of tomatoes with juice, plus water if required, and heat gently. Liquidise this mixture or pass through a sieve, adding a little fresh herb to taste. Drain spaghetti, add hot sauce, 2oz grated cheese and a pinch of oregano herb. Serve with watercress. lettuce or endive.

Tomato and Mushroom Savoury for One

Two medium tomatoes, sliced
4oz mushrooms
A few spring onions
Medium slice of wholemeal bread grated
2oz nuts grated—brazils and walnuts
Fresh herb of choice
Little salt if desired
Oil or vegetable margarine to fry mushrooms

Method:

Place sliced tomatoes in an oiled ovenproof dish; fry the
mushrooms for 2 minutes only and add; with scissors,
snip the spring onions over. Mix the breadcrumbs, nuts,
chopped herb and salt in a basin and add a little oil to
bind. Spread this over the tomato mixture in the dish
and place either under medium grill for ten minutes or
in medium heated oven, if you are already using it for
other dishes. Garnish with watercress.

A few more ideas that don't need recipes

Stuffed tomatoes, green pepper, whole beetroot, baked
jacket potato, raw or baked apple, steamed courgette
or marrow ring, avocado, peach or large flat mushroom;
any of these may be filled with a mixture of rice and beans
with herbs, rice or breadcrumbs and cheese—cream
cheese, cottage or cheddar-type—grated nuts, tomato
and herbs, finely-grated carrots, grated nuts and Tartex
paste or Granose sandwich spread mixed together.

More quick ideas

Try grated raw beetroot, mixed with toasted sesame seeds and chopped parsley, piled on to an avocado half, served on a bed of lettuce or watercress with thin tomato slices. Canned celery hearts, or steamed broccoli spears, with one of the above mixtures on top and put under the grill are quick, too. Canned kidney beans, brown kidney, or haricot beans can be drained and mixed with a salad dressing and other salad items such as tomatoes, cucumber, raw mushrooms and herbs, to make a quick protein dish to go with a green salad.

When wholemeal bread isn't available, try Vitawheat, Ryvita and MacVita crispbreads. Any of these crispbreads, as well as whole cereals like Shredded Wheat, Weetabix etc. are most useful for crushing (broken into a strong polybag, and crushed with a rolling pin) and may be used instead of breadcrumbs in many dishes, sweet and savoury. For instance, crushed Weetabix with a little dark sugar and softened vegetable margarine makes a delicious crumble topping to go on any fruit compote to be baked in the oven. Shredded Wheat crushed can be used in nutroasts, and whole wheat crispbreads are useful for mixing with softened cheese and herbs for party savoury balls.

SOUP OF THE EVENING—BEAUTIFUL SOUP!

Leek and Carrot Soup

2 large carrots diced	4 leeks sliced
1oz butter	1½pts veg. stock or water
Nutmeg	Salt
Chopped parsley	Pepper

Sauté vegetables in butter for 10 minutes without browning. Add stock or water, and cook gently for 30-40 minutes until vegetables are tender. Liquidise all but a cupful, which is left as it is to give texture and colour. Season with nutmeg, salt and pepper, and chopped parsley before serving.

Julienne Soup

2 large onions	Vegetable oil
2 large carrots	Tomato puree
2 or more sticks celery	1½ tsp yeast extract
Other vegetables as	1 bay leaf
available, all washed	2 tbsp chopped fresh chives
and cut into tiny	2pts vegetable stock
pieces about 1″ × ⅛″.	

Soften prepared vegetables in a little vegetable oil, without browning, for about 5 minutes; add hot stock with bayleaf and simmer for about ½ hour. When soup is ready, stir in tomato puree and yeast extract. Sprinkle the chives over the top.

Tomato Soup

¾lb fresh firm tomatoes
1 small onion, bayleaf
   and cloves
2pts vegetable stock

2oz vegetable margarine
Salt, pepper and nutmeg
Pinch of basil

Method:

Gently fry the tomatoes in the margarine until very soft; add the onion, with bayleaf pinned to it with the cloves, and the hot stock. Simmer gently for about 20 minutes; add salt, pepper and nutmeg. Remove onion, liquidise soup or pass through a sieve, add basil, and gently re-heat if necessary. Serve with either finely-chopped parsley or other fresh herb snipped on top—or a few washed celery leaves or watercress leaves.

Minty Green Pea Soup

8oz split green peas
2 large carrots, finely
   chopped
2oz vegetable margarine
1 tbsp chopped mint leaves

2 large onions, finely chopped
2pts vegetable stock
1½ tsp yeast extract

Method:

Wash peas and soak in plenty of water for at least 12 hours. Cook in this water over a low heat until tender, which will take 2 hours at least; add more liquid if necessary. Melt margarine in second large pan, add onions and carrots; cook without browning for 5 minutes. Add hot vegetable stock, bring to the boil and simmer for 10 minutes. Add the cooked peas, mashed or sieved, and mint. Stir well whilst reheating; and add yeast extract just before serving.

FRESH AND TANGY STARTERS

Dessert apple slices sprinkled with orange juice and powdered ginger.

Peeled and sliced orange and banana, sprinkled with a little cinnamon.

Juicy William pears stuffed with softened dates.

Sliced strawberries and cucumber.

Thinly-sliced peeled oranges, tomatoes and onion rings.

Pineapple ring on top of coarse-grated carrot, and sprigs of watercress.

Melon portions scattered with fresh redcurrants.

Grated dessert apple and grated raw or cooked beetroot on a bed of lettuce, watercress or mustard and cress.

Fresh grapefruit and orange sections with toasted hazelnuts.

Grated raw turnip and carrot, onion rings and toasted sesame seeds, garnished with finely-chopped parsley.

Sliced raw mushrooms and tomatoes on chopped lettuce.

Grated celeriac, chopped tomatoes and any kind of cooked beans, garden peas or chick peas, with mint, savory or basil.

Finely-chopped cabbage—red, white or green—with caraway seeds in an oil and lemon dressing, with strips of red pepper.

Chopped raw brussels sprouts and sliced tomatoes with dressing.

Raw cauliflower florets with carrot and cucumber sticks.

Tartex paste, or other savoury spread, on toast squares or bran biscuits with chopped chives.

YOUR EVENING MEAL

Here is a selection of savouries and composite meals, to be served with either a salad or fresh short-cooked vegetables, always including a green one.

Sesame and Brazilnut Roast (for four)

6oz coarse-grated Brazils
2oz sesame seeds
3oz wholemeal breadcrumbs
1oz rolled oats
1oz wholemeal flour
1 large onion finely chopped
2 large tomatoes chopped
1½oz corn oil
¼pt vegetable stock
1 tbsp fresh chopped herbs or 1 tsp dried herbs
1 rounded tsp yeast extract

Method:

Fry onion in oil gently for 5 minutes and then add tomatoes. Stir in 1oz flour, carefully add hot vegetable stock in which yeast extract has been dissolved; simmer whilst stirring for about 3 minutes. Add this mixture to all dry ingredients in a large bowl and mix well. Put in oiled ovenproof dish or loaf tin, with a layer of stuffing if desired, and bake in centre of oven for 30-40 minutes at 375° or Gas Mark 5.

Tomato and Celery Stuffing

Lightly fry three chopped stalks of celery and two chopped tomatoes in 1oz vegetable margarine for 10 minutes. Press this stuffing between the two layers of nut roast. Lightly fried mushrooms and diced cooked beetroot would also make a suitable stuffing.

Chick Peas with Brown Rice (for three)

6oz whole-grain rice	3 tbsp corn oil
1 large onion chopped	1 tsp dried herbs
1pt hot vegetable stock	4oz mushrooms chopped
3 large tomatoes chopped	2 peppers (1 red, 1 green)
5 inch piece cucumber	chopped
chopped	

6oz chick peas, soaked 24 hours and cooked for 2 hours at simmer point. (Chick peas do not go mushy)

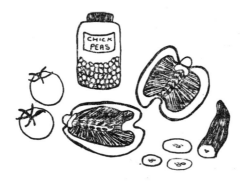

Method:

Cook onion and washed rice in the oil for 5 minutes; carefully pour in the hot stock and simmer for 15 minutes. Add all other ingredients and simmer another 20 minutes, seasoning to taste. This recipe may also be used with any kind of cooked beans, instead of the chick peas. Roughly-chopped cashews or walnuts can be added at the end of cooking.

Cauliflower Noisette

Place cooked cauliflower florets in an oiled ovenproof dish and scatter 2oz grated cheese per portion over the top. Brown in hot oven for a few minutes. Garnish with tomato wedges and finely-chopped parsley.

Golden Slice (for four)

5oz rolled oats
6oz grated cheddar cheese
2 large carrots grated
1 rounded tbsp soya flour mixed with 4 tbsp milk
2oz vegetable margarine
Salt, pepper, pinch of thyme or rosemary.

Method:
Melt margarine in large pan, remove from heat, mix in all other ingredients, stir well, press into an oiled ovenproof dish and bake for 25 minutes at 375°F or Gas Mark 5.

Nutty Crisp (for two)

2oz Weetabix or Shredded Wheat
2oz vegetable margarine
4oz grated brazil nuts or mixed nuts
1 small finely chopped onion
Pinch dried herbs or 1 dessp fresh herbs
1 rounded tsp yeast extract
Little hot water if necessary

Method:
Melt margarine, add yeast extract, stir well; then add all other ingredients and hot water if necessary. Press into an oiled ovenproof dish and bake for 15 minutes at 400°F or Gas Mark 6. For a change, half the cereal for this dish could be oats.

Savoury Peppers (for two)

Cook washed whole green peppers in a little water for 10 minutes. Cool, cut off top slice, remove seeds. Fill with mixture of 2oz cooked brown rice, chopped tomatoes, 4oz grated cheese or 4oz grated mixed nuts, seasoning and herbs. Replace "lid", put into an oiled ovenproof dish and cook for about 35 minutes at 350°F or Gas Mark 4.

Millet and Tomato Savoury (for four)

1 medium finely-chopped onion
½pt tomato juice
2 sticks finely-chopped celery
2 chopped tomatoes
4oz grated mixed nuts
Chopped parsley to serve

1oz oil or margarine
6oz washed millet
Bayleaf
1 medium apple grated
Celery seed
Coriander

Method:

Fry onion in the oil for 4 minutes. Add tomato juice, millet and bayleaf; simmer on low heat until thick—about 15 minutes. Take from heat, remove bayleaf, stir in all other ingredients and place in oiled ovenproof dish; dot with a little extra margarine and bake for about 35 minutes at 375°F or Gas Mark 5. Sprinkle with chopped parsley to serve. Can also be made with a 14oz tin of tomatoes instead of juice and tomatoes.

Lentil and Tomato Bake (for four)

8oz lentils
Small onion, bayleaf and cloves
2 dessp finely-chopped parsley

14oz tin tomatoes, or ½lb fresh and ½pt water
2 medium carrots grated
Large pinch mace
Pinch salt
1½oz vegetable margarine

Method

Wash lentils, add to pan with carrots, tomatoes and studded onion, bring to boil, turn down very low, put on tight-fitting lid, leave for 25 minutes. Remove onion (can be used for soup), add all other ingredients, mixing well with a wooden spoon. Turn into a greased loaf tin, dot the top with a little margarine and bake for 30 minutes at 375°F or Gas Mark 5. Turn out and decorate if required.

Uncooked Nut Savouries

6oz finely-grated mixed nuts
2oz wholemeal breadcrumbs
1 small finely-chopped onion or celery
3 tbsp hot vegetable stock. (Use left-over vegetable cooking water, or hot water with dissolved vegetable stock cube)

Method:
Pour hot stock over crumbs, leave 20 minutes. Add most of nuts, all onion, and mix to a stiff paste. Roll into balls and coat with rest of nuts. Chill for an hour.

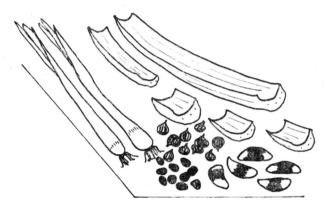

Cheese, Apple and Beetroot Flan (for four)

8oz strong cheddar cheese grated
1 large apple grated
1 large cooked beetroot grated
1 rounded tsp ground coriander
$\frac{1}{2}$ tsp celery seeds

Method:
Put all grated items into a bowl, add coriander and celery seeds, mix well. Spoon into flan dish lined with wholemeal pastry (see page 46), press down gently, cook at 375°F or Gas Mark 5 for 25-30 minutes.

Cheese Bites

8oz cream cheese
2 tsp finely-grated onion
2 tsp finely-chopped
parsley
1 tsp finely-chopped chives
1½oz finely-minced peanuts or hazels

1 tbsp sweet chutney
Salt and pepper
Dash paprika pepper

Method:

Mix all ingredients except nuts and paprika. Shape into balls, roll into nuts and paprika. Chill well and serve with salad or on little sticks for parties.

Hungarian Bean Loaf (for four)

8oz butter beans soaked
overnight
1 chopped green pepper
2 tbsp fresh chopped
parsley

1 chopped onion
1 crushed clove garlic
2 tbsp vegetable oil
Sea salt and paprika

Method:

Cook butter beans on a simmering heat for about 2 hours; drain well, and sieve or liquidise to purée. Sweat onion, garlic and pepper in oil. Mix all together, season to taste, and bake in a moderate oven at 375°F or Gas Mark 5 for about 35 minutes, until golden. Turn out and decorate with slices of tomato and lemon twists.

Mushroom Roast (for four)

8oz sliced mushrooms
1 large onion chopped
4oz wholemeal
breadcrumbs
3oz vegetable margarine
2 tbsp chopped parsley

8oz grated cheddar cheese
1 small green pepper chopped
2 chopped tomatoes
Pinch of mixed herbs
Seasoning to taste

Method:

Gently fry onion and pepper in margarine, add mushrooms, cook for 1 minute more. Remove from heat, add remaining ingredients except for 2oz cheese. Mix well, fill oiled ovenproof dish with the mixture, scatter the remaining cheese on top. Bake on middle shelf of oven at 350°F or Gas Mark 4 for 30 minutes.

Mushroom Pizza (for four)

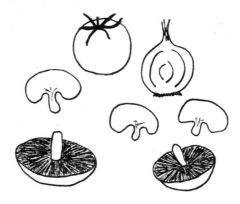

8oz plain wholemeal flour
2 tsp baking powder
A little over $\frac{1}{4}$pt of milk
Two large onions
Oil for frying
1 extra dessp flour

6 large tomatoes or 14oz tin
8oz grated cheese
6oz lightly-fried mushrooms
Oregano herb, salt and
 pepper
$\frac{1}{4}$pt hot vegetable stock (if
 using fresh tomatoes)

Method:

Mix flour and baking powder together; make a well in centre, pour in some of the milk and mix to soft dough, only adding more milk if necessary. Press dough into a baking tin with $1\frac{1}{2}$ inch sides, which has been brushed with oil. Fry onions in oil gently for 3 minutes, add the dessertspoonful of flour, mix well, and slowly add the $\frac{1}{4}$ pint of hot stock; simmer to thicken. Add the chopped tomatoes and about a quarter of the grated cheese; stir gently off the heat, then pour on to dough. Scatter the rest of the cheese over, also the chopped or whole mushrooms and the oregano. Bake at 425°F or Gas Mark 7 for about 20 minutes. Serve hot or cold. When making this with tinned tomatoes, use the 'juice' instead of hot stock.

Peanut Chowder (for four)

1 large onion finely
   chopped
2 tbsp vegetable oil
1 level tbsp wholemeal
   flour

3 large tbsp peanut butter
$\frac{3}{4}$pt vegetable stock
$\frac{1}{2}$pt milk
Seasoning to taste

1 medium tin celery hearts chopped (or fresh cooked
   celery)
4oz grated cheddar cheese

Method:

Fry onion in the oil until soft; stir in flour and peanut
butter. Gradually blend in stock and milk, bring to boil,
stir well until thickened. Lower heat, add chopped
celery, seasoning and chopped fresh herb to taste, and
last of all the grated cheese. Allow the cheese to melt,
and serve with crusty wholemeal bread.

COMPLEMENTARY SAUCES

Red Pepper Sauce

2 large red peppers, seeds removed and finely-chopped
1 garlic clove crushed
1 medium sized onion finely-chopped
1 stalk of celery finely-chopped
3 tbsp oil
½pt vegetable stock   3 tbsp tomato purée
Salt, black pepper and cayenne to taste

Method:

Heat oil, cook garlic and onion for 5 minutes. Add peppers and celery, cook further 5 minutes. Add hot stock, stir well, bringing to boil. Rub through wire sieve or purée in a blender. Return to heat, add tomato purée, salt, pepper and cayenne; stir, keep hot until ready to serve.

Savoury Mushroom Sauce

1 tbsp fine oatmeal   1 heaped tsp yeast extract
1 tbsp soya flour   ½pt hot vegetable stock
1 tbsp vegetable oil
¼lb finely-chopped and lightly fried mushrooms
Other seasoning to taste

Method:

In a saucepan mix oatmeal and soya flour with a little cold water to produce a thick cream. Add yeast extract and oil, stir well, and gradually add stock. Bring to the boil and cook for 2 minutes. Add mushrooms and season to taste.

WINNING WAYS WITH VEGETABLES

There must be hundreds of different ways of serving vegetables to make them taste good and look attractive. Here are just a few.

Brussels Sprouts with Mushrooms

1lb trimmed washed brussels sprouts
1oz vegetable oil and 1oz vegetable margarine
4oz chopped mushrooms

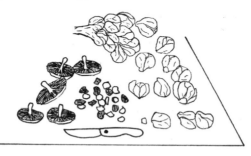

Method:
Steam the prepared sprouts in a basket inside a pan with a little water till almost tender. Toss the mushrooms in the heated oil and margarine for 4 minutes and add the sprouts to the pan when ready, stir and serve garnished with chopped parsley.

Beetroots a la Turque

1lb cooked peeled beetroots
1 dessp chives
2 small pots natural yoghourt
1 saltspoon each of cinnamon, nutmeg and pepper
Method:
Heat beetroots in a little water in a covered pan. Strain and slice into an oiled ovenproof dish. Mix all other ingredients in a basin and pour over beetroot, cover and place in medium oven for 20 minutes. This is delicious served with nutroast and a green vegetable lightly steamed.

Chinese Leaves with Walnut and Muscatel Sauce

1lb Chinese Leaves	3oz muscatel raisins
6oz orange juice	1oz chopped walnuts
1 tbsp lemon juice	2 level tsp arrowroot

Method:

Slice the cabbage lengthwise once, wash well, and place in steamer or steaming basket with an inch or so of water. Steam for 15-20 minutes. (Make sure that pan does not run dry.) Soak muscatels in the orange juice for 2 hours, drain and set aside. Mix the arrowroot powder with a little of the orange juice in a cup to a smooth paste. Put the rest of the juice and the lemon juice into a small pan and heat, adding the paste and stirring well at boiling point for 2 minutes. Add muscatels and chopped walnuts, and pour over Chinese leaves arranged in a hot dish.

More Ways with Vegetables

Steamed garden peas can be served tossed in a little vegetable margarine, add fresh chives snipped over them, as a change from mint.

Steamed small chopped cabbage, tossed in a little vegetable margarine and sprinkled with caraway seeds.

Steamed cabbage mixed with fried onions and tomatoes and a little basil sprinkled over.

Steamed celery hearts placed in an oiled ovenproof dish, sprinkled with wholemeal breadcrumbs and grated cheese mixed with a crushed garlic clove, then grilled for a few minutes.

Steamed garden peas mixed with a little melted vegetable margarine, finely-chopped onion and a little grated well-washed orange peel.

Jacket baked potatoes lend themselves to many variations. Scrub a large potato, make a few holes with a fork to allow steam to escape, and bake for 1 to 2 hours at a medium heat. When cooked, they can be split open and cheese, tomatoes, onion slices etc. inserted; return to the oven for a few minutes.

SALADS FOR VITALITY AND VARIETY

Avocado and Orange Salad

Arrange a bed of lettuce or chicory leaves on a plate. Skin and stone a ripe avocado pear, and cut slices about ¾ inch thick. Remove all skin, pips and pith from a large orange, and separate into slices. Place alternate slices of orange and avocado in a pattern round the dish, heap cress in the centre, and sprinkle a little oil and lemon dressing over.

Mushroom, Bean and Melon Salad

Peel and remove the seeds from a small honeydew melon and cut into 1 inch cubes. Drain a can of red kidney beans, and slice 4oz button mushrooms. Mix all ingredients with several tablespoonfuls of yoghourt dressing. Serve on a dish of lettuce or chicory.

Carrot, Onion and Beetroot Salad

6 large cooked carrots diced, mixed with 2 large cooked beetroots diced, several chopped spring onions and a dressing made from 1 rounded teaspoon creamed horseradish sauce and a little milk mixed together. Spoon mixture on to a dish of watercress, and sprinkle on chopped fresh herb of choice.

Runner Bean and Tomato Salad

8oz lightly-steamed runner beans, 8oz sliced tomatoes, 3 inches cucumber diced, lemon and oil dressing, and parsley. Place runner beans, tomatoes and cucumber into a shallow bowl, pour over dressing and sprinkle with parsley. Allow to marinate for 30 minutes before serving.

Cheese and Radish Salad

Trim washed radishes and slice across thinly, dice about 4 inches of cucumber and a small dessert apple, cut firm cheddar cheese into dice. Mix all these items together with either yoghourt dressing or oil and lemon dressing. Spoon on to a bed of cress and sprinkle a little dried dill herb over.

Celery Coleslaw

Wash and trim one large celery head, shred about ½lb white cabbage, chop two firm tomatoes, finely-chop 1 large onion and half a small green pepper. Toss all these items in oil and lemon dressing, adding freshly ground pepper or a pinch of mustard powder to the dressing, if desired.

Walnut, Apple and Orange Salad

Remove all skin, pips and pith from a large orange, cut into slices or separate into sections. Dice two red dessert apples and chop two sticks of celery. Toss all items with 2oz shelled walnuts in a lemon and oil or yoghourt dressing, and spoon on to a bed of lettuce or chicory.

Winter Salad

Finely shred ½lb washed brussels sprouts or inner cabbage leaves, shred one medium onion, grate one small washed turnip (trim only, leave skin on) and 3 medium carrots. Mix all items with yoghourt dressing or oil and lemon dressing with seasoning and a pinch of dried herbs.

Celeriac Salad

Wash, trim and finely grate a celeriac root, and mix with 3 medium carrots coarsely-grated, 1 medium onion finely-chopped, and half a bunch of watercress chopped. Toss in yoghourt dressing or oil and lemon dressing.

Fennel and Cucumber Salad

Wash, trim and finely slice one small fennel head, mix with 4 inches washed diced cucumber and $\frac{1}{2}$lb cooked garden peas. Toss in yoghourt dressing or oil and lemon dressing.

Apricot Salad

Soak $\frac{1}{2}$lb washed apricot halves (dried) in $\frac{1}{4}$ pint of orange juice overnight. Drain and place carefully on a bed of lettuce. Arrange slices of fresh orange—peel, pips and pith removed—and scatter with chopped brazil nuts.

Curried Cauliflower Salad

Wash a small cauliflower, break into florets, allow to drain well. Slice thinly and mix with $\frac{1}{2}$lb scrubbed carrots very thinly sliced. Make a dressing of 2 level teaspoons of curry paste (ready made from a jar) carefully mixed into a lemon and oil dressing, and toss the cauliflower and carrot mixture in this. Serve on a bed of watercress, garnished with tomato wedges.

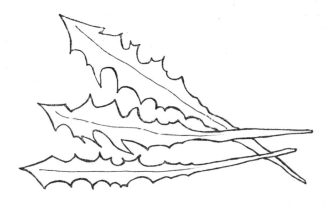

Dandelion Salad

Pick fresh young dandelion leaves from centre top of plant (from place where no sprays are used) and wash well; shred finely and mix with chopped spring onions, thinly sliced cucumber and two firm tomatoes coarsely-chopped. Toss in oil and lemon dressing and sprinkle with finely-chopped parsley.

Raisin and Walnut Salad

Steam 4oz brown rice until cooked and allow to cool. Soak 2oz washed raisins in a little orange juice for 1-2 hours, drain. Chop one large banana and one large tomato; mix these with the cooled rice, raisins, and 2oz shelled walnut halves. Pour over either yoghourt dressing or oil and lemon dressing with a little freshly chopped mint mixed in.

Brown Rice and Cashewnut Salad

Steam 4oz brown rice until cooked—allow to cool. Chop two firm tomatoes, dice a small piece of green pepper; mix these with the cooled rice and 2oz washed whole or broken cashews. Stir in oil and lemon dressing and, using scissors, snip chives and chervil over the top.

Broad Bean and Carrot Salad

Mix $\frac{1}{2}$lb shelled and cooked broad beans (or canned and drained), 4 sticks of chopped celery, a piece of green or red pepper chopped and three medium carrots, scrubbed and coarsely grated, into an oil and lemon dressing.

SALAD DRESSINGS

Yoghourt Dressing

5oz carton natural yoghourt
1 tsp finely-chopped mint or herbs of choice
Little salt and freshly-ground pepper if desired
2 tsp of freshly-squeezed lemon juice

Method:

Mix all ingredients together. It is best used the same day as made, but it may be kept in refrigerator for several hours.

Oil and Lemon Dressing

2 tbsp freshly-squeezed lemon juice
6 tbsp vegetable oil
Pinch of salt and/or little sugar, if desired

Method:

Pour all ingredients into a 1lb glass jar with screw-top lid firmly placed and shake well. Keep in a refrigerator or very cold place and use within 2-3 days.

MUESLI

—for breakfast or when you are rushed off your feet and think that you haven't time for a square meal. Muesli, carefully made, can be a good nourishing meal—eaten by old or young alike at any time of day.

Ingredients for one person:

1 tbsp rolled oats or mixed muesli base
1 tbsp grated nuts (fine, medium or coarse grated)
1 tbsp seedless raisins (soaked in water or juice)
1 medium dessert apple grated
A little dark sugar or molasses to taste
Milk or plantmilk, water or fruit juice to mix.

Method:

Mix all ingredients in a basin using just enough chosen liquid to make a soft mixture.

A little lemon juice may be added and any soaked, dried fruit as well as fresh-chopped or grated fruit in season, to make variety all the year round. For instance, in the summer soft fruit season, make a strawberry, peach, raspberry, redcurrant or blackberry muesli— delicious! A dessertspoonful of wheatgerm or natural bran can be stirred in as well if required.

DELICIOUS DESSERTS FOR YOUR CONSIDERATION

Home-made yoghourt

Heat one pint of milk to near boiling point, withdraw from heat, and stand by to test with absolutely clean finger (unless you have a cook's thermometer) to determine when it has dropped to blood temperature.

Have ready a warmed wide-neck Thermos flask. Mix 1 tablespoon of ready-made yoghourt with the milk in the pan, pour into the flask and seal down. Leave for four hours. This can then be mixed with herbs and used as a salad dressing, or with fruit as a dessert. If it is to be kept for a day or so, it must be emptied into a clean basin, allowed to cool, then covered and placed in a refrigerator.

Baked Apples with Dates or Sultanas

Wash and core large Bramley apples and incise a ring around the fruit with a pointed knife. Place in an oven-proof dish with $\frac{1}{2}$ inch of water. Fill centres of apples tightly with chopped dates or sultanas, with a little dark sugar if required. Brush all over apple with a little vegetable oil and bake at 350°F or Gas Mark 4 for about an hour.

Raisins or chopped soaked dried banana could also be used as fillings. The addition of a little nutmeg, ginger or cinnamon makes them more delicious.

Cashewnut Cream

4oz finely-ground cashewnuts, 6 tbsp water, 2oz soaked, chopped dates or raw cane sugar to taste. Mix all in a blender till smooth.

Fruit Jelly

Put two rounded teaspoons of powdered agar agar into a basin with two tablespoons of cold water, mix and let stand ten minutes. Pour on $\frac{1}{2}$ pint boiling water, stir well, and pour back into saucepan. Boil for one minute stirring well. Remove from heat, pour in $\frac{1}{2}$ pint of orange or pineapple juice, stir well and add chopped pieces of fruit before pouring into a fancy mould or individual dishes. Try cashewnut cream with it (see page 43).

Apricot Delight

Soak 8oz dried apricots overnight in about $\frac{1}{2}$ pint orange juice. Rub through a sieve, or liquidise, and spoon into a large bowl or individual dishes. Decorate with desiccated coconut around the edge and pistachios sliced and scattered over.

BAKING WITH WHOLEMEAL FLOUR

Wholemeal Fruit Scones

$\frac{3}{4}$lb plain wholemeal flour
2 heaped tsp baking
  powder
2oz vegetable oil or
  margarine

Pinch salt
2oz soft brown sugar
4oz dried fruit
Grated rind $\frac{1}{2}$ lemon
Milk to mix

Method:

Mix flour, salt and baking powder; rub in fat. Make a hollow and put in sugar, lemon rind and $\frac{1}{2}$ cup milk. Mix to a soft dough, using a little more milk if necessary. Lastly mix in the dried fruit. Put dough on to a floured board and lightly press down to $\frac{3}{4}$ inch depth; use scone cutter to make rounds, and place them fairly close to each other on an oiled baking tray. Brush with milk, let stand 10 minutes, and bake in hot oven, 400°F or Gas Mark 6 for 12-15 minutes.

Cheese and Watercress Scones

8oz plain wholemeal flour
2 rounded tsp baking
  powder
$\frac{1}{2}$ tsp salt
4-5 tbsp milk

2oz vegetable margarine
3oz grated Cheddar cheese
$1\frac{1}{2}$ bunches well washed,
  finely-chopped watercress

Method:

Mix flour, salt and baking powder; rub in margarine. Stir in cheese and cress and mix in milk for a soft dough. Knead lightly on a floured board and roll out to an inch thick; cut out 3" wide rounds or squares and place on a well-oiled baking tray, fairly close together as this will make them rise. Brush tops with a little milk, and bake for about 15 minutes at 425°F or Gas Mark 7.

Wholemeal Pastry

6oz wholemeal flour
½ level tsp salt

3oz vegetable fat or
vegetable margarine
About 2 tbsp cold water

Method:

Mix flour and salt, and rub in fat to breadcrumb stage. Add water very gradually, and gather together into one firm piece. Leave in the basin, cover and put in the refrigerator for 30 minutes. Roll out on to a floured board to size and shape required, using a little flour from dredger if required. The resulting pastry is sufficient for an 8 inch flan case or 4 individual tins of about 4 inch diameter.

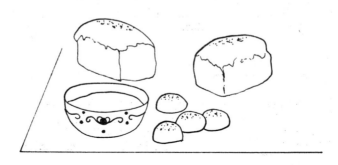

Wholemeal Bread (two 1lb loaves and 4 small rolls)

2lb wholemeal flour   1pt warm water
1 level tsp sugar   1 level tbsp dried yeast
1 dessp malt extract   1 level dessp salt

Method:

Measure 2lb flour into a large bowl, cover with a cloth and put in a warm place. Put sugar and dried yeast into a measuring jug and pour in $\frac{1}{2}$pt water, tested at blood-heat with clean finger. Stir, cover and put in a warm place. Stir the salt and malt extract into the other $\frac{1}{2}$pt water, cover and put in a warm place. When yeast has become really frothy (15-20 minutes) make a well in the centre of the flour and pour in the salt and malt mixture and the yeast mixture. Mix well by hand. Turn out on to a floured board and knead for about 3 minutes, until you feel the dough change consistency. Divide into 2 large pieces, leaving enough over for about 4 small rolls. Put each large piece into an oiled tin and divide the remaining dough into 4. Roll in floured hands and place on an oiled tray. Cover all tins with a clean dry cloth and put back in warm place for as long as it takes for them to double in size. Place at the top of the oven at 400°F for 10 minutes and then reduce to 350° for a further 30-40 minutes. When the bread is properly cooked, the loaves should sound hollow when tapped underneath.

Rolls need to be removed from the oven after 10-15 minutes. Turn out on to a wire tray and leave to cool out of a draught.

WHERE CAN I TURN FOR HELP?

The Vegetarian Society of course!

In return for a large self-addressed envelope with two second-class postage stamps you will be sent free literature which includes a book list, recipes and a copy of the magazine 'Alive'. The Society also operates a free information service on vegetarian matters.

'Alive' brings you news, views, recipes, articles on ecology, health, animal welfare, self-sufficiency and organic gardening.

Information on vegetarian restaurants, hotels and guest houses, health food stores, health centres and hydros, and food additives, can be found in the Society's International Vegetarian Healthfood Handbook, which also contains a Shoppers' Guide section listing a wide range of products acceptable to vegetarians along with other details which are invaluable not just for vegetarians but for everyone concerned with healthy eating.

Write to: The Vegetarian Society (UK) Limited
Parkdale
Dunham Road
Altrincham
Cheshire WA14 4QG

or: The Vegetarian Centre & Bookshop
53 Marloes Road
Kensington
London W8 6LA

We welcome visitors to our Bookshop where they can browse through our extensive range of titles at their leisure.